PRESERVING FAMILY LANDS

ESSENTIAL TAX STRATEGIES FOR THE LANDOWNER

STEPHEN J. SMALL
Attorney at Law

Landowner Planning Center
Boston, Massachusetts

The purpose of this book is to alert landowners to the nature and extent of potential tax and land-saving problems that may face them and their families, and to suggest possible solutions. No reader should undertake any of the suggestions described in this book without first consulting competent professional advisors.

Tax and family land planning is an individual and personal matter for each landowner and for each family. Current financial circumstances and long-term financial goals differ, as do relationships between family members and different generations. Any single book cannot be, and this one is not intended to be, a substitute for individual tax and legal advice and planning.

Copyright© 1992 by Stephen J. Small, Esq.

All rights reserved.

Preserving Family Lands is a registered trademark.

Second Edition

First Edition Published 1988

Design: BECK designs, Debra M. Beck

Cover: Christine Kidder Griffin

Printed in the United States of America

Library of Congress Catalog Card Number: 92-85506

ISBN 0-9624557-1-7

Landowner Planning Center
P.O. Box 4508
Boston, MA 02101-4508
(617) 357-1644

Special bulk rates for the purchase of *Preserving Family Lands–Essential Tax Strategies for the Landowner* are available for tax-exempt organizations and government agencies. Write to the Landowner Planning Center for details.

If you would like to be on the Landowner Planning Center mailing list for announcements about publications and other information, please write to us and let us know.

Table of Contents

Introduction to the Second Edition

In 1988, I wrote *Preserving Family Lands* as a response to what I saw as a need for more simple, easy-to-read, basic literature about protecting the family's land. The book discussed some of the options that are available to landowners, and the tax consequences associated with those options. I used a small number of examples to illustrate possible tax and land-planning problems and some of the possibilities that may be open to readers. What I tried to do was to cover *as simply as possible* a lot of the preliminary issues and questions that come up when a landowner begins to think about preserving his or her land.

I had no idea what a need there was!! The first edition, published in May of 1988, sold more than 50,000 copies, in all fifty states and even abroad!! *Some readers have told me that this is the most important book in its field in at least the past decade.*

The time has come to revise and update *Preserving Family Lands*. While much of the text is the same, this second edition includes current income tax rates and estate tax rates and other revisions based on tax law changes over the past five years. I have also made some editorial changes and some design changes, including using wider margins so readers will have room to add notes, comments, and questions. I think this will be especially helpful for readers who plan to sit down with their advisors to begin some of the planning discussed in this book.

As with the first edition, there are a number of things this book will not do. It will not go into the intricacies of the income tax or the estate tax. It will not go into all types of charitable giving. It will not cover all of the state and Federal incentives and programs that are available to landowners, either in the tax law or through other means, to help preserve the family farm or ranch. It will not tell you how to convince reluctant family members to protect the family's land and save taxes, although it will give you information and ideas that may help you if such convincing becomes necessary. This book will not discuss all of the planning options and will not answer all of your questions.

This book also does not separately cover a simple, outright gift of land to charity, although the tax rules that apply to such a gift are covered here. However, there are quite a few things this book *will* do. It will give you information about land-saving choices. It will give you information about how you can combine saving land with saving taxes. It will help you find the right advisors if you decide to go ahead with preserving your family's land, and it will help you ask those advisors the right questions.

I would like to thank all of the people and all of the groups around the country who purchased the first edition of *Preserving Family Lands*. I would like to thank all of the readers who have written to me with letters of thanks for helping them to preserve their own important land and for enabling them to pass the word on to others about how to help preserve the quality of life in their communities. And, once again, I would like to thank my wife Connie and my daughters Stephanie and Victoria for their continued support.

S.J.S.

What Happens If...

The chart below summarizes in very brief form what happens to John and Mary and their property, Riverview, under different possibilities discussed in this book.

What Happens if John and Mary:	Income Tax Savings?	Estate Tax Savings?	What happens to Riverview?
Leave Riverview to the children in their wills (Chapter 1)	No	No! Catastrophe!!	Forced sale for development
Make a gift to charity now of an easement on Riverview, and then leave Riverview to the children (Chapter 3)	Yes	Yes	Riverview goes to the children and will be protected
Make a gift to charity now of a remainder interest in Riverview (Chapter 4)	Yes	Yes	Riverview goes to charity and will be protected
Make a gift to charity of Riverview, or of an easement on Riverview, in their wills (Chapter 5)	No	Yes	Riverview will be protected
Give Riverview to the children now (Chapter 6)	No	Yes	Riverview might be protected
Sell Riverview now, for cash (Chapter 7)	No!!	No!!!	Sold for development

CHAPTER 1

The Estate Tax:
An Eye-Opener

John and Mary and Riverview

John and Mary Landowner are very lucky people. Twenty-five years ago they bought Riverview, a 200-acre estate, for $100,000. The value of Riverview crept up steadily for fifteen years after that and skyrocketed in the past decade.

John and Mary are in their sixties now, and they love the quiet at Riverview, the gently rolling hills and open fields. Although Riverview lies in the path of increasing suburban sprawl, the Landowners would like to see their property permanently protected. A developer recently offered them $2,500,000 for Riverview, but they turned him down. The land is too important to them to sell out, and they are planning to leave Riverview to their children, along with the $2 million in other assets John and Mary have accumulated.

The Landowners both have wills, drawn up some years ago. Under their wills, the first to die leaves everything to the survivor, and, on the death of the second spouse, the children inherit the estate. Let's see what happens.

Let's assume that John dies first. Under the Federal estate tax laws, there is little or no Federal estate tax due at that time. When Mary dies, these are the results, keeping in mind that she has Riverview, worth $2,500,000 (likely to be worth more than that because of future appreciation), and $2 million in other assets:

- The Federal estate tax on her $4,500,000 estate is $1,587,400. In addition, if the Landowners lived in Massachusetts, the Massachusetts estate tax would be $625,500. Total tax due? $2,212,900!!!

- *Riverview must be sold to pay the estate tax.* The estate tax is due nine months after Mary's death, so the family may not even be able to wait for the "best offer."

- Once Riverview is sold for development, the gently rolling hills and open fields will be gone forever. *The future of Riverview is completely out of the hands of the family.*

Bob and Sue and Diamond Farm

Bob and Sue Farmowner own Diamond Farm, 500 acres that Bob's father bought in the 1940's for $50 an acre that has been farmed by the family since that time. All of the family's energy, and almost all of the family's cash, has been poured into the farm. In addition to Diamond Farm, they have about $200,000 in cash and stocks, most of that inherited from Sue's parents.

Bob and Sue are in their late fifties now. They know there are other things they could do that might make life a little easier for them (they have been offered $1,500,000 for Diamond Farm by a local real estate developer), but they are proud of their way of life and what they have been able to build up. It gives them a lot of pride, too, to know that their children want the farm to stay in the family so they can follow in Bob and Sue's footsteps. Bob and Sue certainly don't feel like millionaires, but their prime agricultural land on the urban fringe puts them into that category.

Under their wills, drawn up some years ago, the first to die leaves everything to the survivor, and, on the death of the second spouse, the children inherit Diamond Farm. Let's see what happens. (There is a special Federal estate tax assessment program for farms, and Diamond Farm and the Farmowners' estate might be eligible. The purpose of this example, however, is to point out the awful result that occurs if that program is not available or not used, or if a family is unwilling or unable to continue to farm the whole property.)

Let's assume that Sue dies first. Under the Federal estate tax laws, there is little or no Federal estate tax due at that time. When Bob dies, he thinks he leaves Diamond Farm and the $200,000 in other assets to the children. This is what happens:

- The Federal estate tax on his $1,700,000 estate is $375,000. In addition, if the Farmowners lived in

Colorado, or Virginia, or Florida, for example, the estate tax due to the state would be $78,000. Total tax due? $453,000!!!

- *Diamond Farm must be sold to pay the estate tax.* The estate tax is due nine months after Bob's death, so the family may be forced to take less than they expect.

- Once Diamond Farm is sold for development, one more fertile, working farm will be gone forever, along with its contribution to the nation's food and fiber and its contribution to the region's open space. The future of Diamond Farm is completely out of the hands of the family.

You May Have a Problem, But You Also Have Choices

Most people certainly aren't as comfortable as John and Mary and certainly don't have land as valuable as Riverview. Most people don't have land as valuable as Diamond Farm, either. *But I use these examples to illustrate the awful and devastating effect the estate tax system can have on a family's land and a family's plans.*

This book will make two important points. The first point is that many of you, like the families I have mentioned, are facing a potentially significant *estate tax* problem, because in many cases, a major portion of your estate is a *very valuable* piece of land. Even if you have property that is significantly less valuable than Riverview or Diamond Farm, you still may be facing the same problem.

FOR THE FIRST TIME IN THE HISTORY OF THE UNITED STATES, THE FAMILY THAT JUST WANTS TO LEAVE ITS LAND TO THE CHILDREN MAY NOT BE ABLE TO DO THAT. The land may have become so valuable it may have to be sold to pay the estate tax.

The second point is that there is, in fact, something you can do about this problem. You do have choices.

CHAPTER 2

Where Do We Begin?

The Problem

We can begin with an understanding of the problem.

Simply put, the problem is this: without proper planning, a valuable piece of land in an estate can trigger an estate tax so large that the land itself will have to be sold to pay the estate tax. If it is important for the family to preserve the land and to have a manageable estate tax bill, the lack of proper planning can lead to a terrible and irreversible result.

For the community that cares about protecting the quality of life, the Federal estate tax may be the biggest single threat to the protection of farmland and forestland, watershed, open space, wildlife habitat, and scenic vistas. FOR THE FAMILY THAT CARES ABOUT ITS LAND, THE FEDERAL ESTATE TAX MAY BE THE BIGGEST SINGLE THREAT TO THE FAMILY'S LONG-RANGE PLANNING.

Why does this potential problem exist for so many families today? I think there are four reasons.

First, the dramatic increase in land values, particularly over the past decades, has added wealth, in some cases enormous wealth, to many families. Bob and Sue Farmowner are only one example of thousands of families that are now land rich and cash poor, heading for a major estate tax shock and setback.

Second, while Federal income tax rates have generally dropped, Federal *estate tax rates* remain high, and are now especially high when compared to Federal income tax rates. The highest effective Federal estate tax rate is above 50%; the highest effective Federal income tax rate is now approximately 31%. All of the explosive appreciation in Riverview continues to be taxed at a *very high* estate tax rate.

Third, part of the "problem" is that an increasing number of families want to protect the family's land. The family land conservation ethic wasn't quite so strong when it was easier to find a pretty, tranquil place to live, or a desirable ranch or farm, when so many nice pieces of property had not yet fallen victim to the bulldozer and the subdivision. How many times have John and Mary Landowner said or thought, "Why, we couldn't find another place like this one, and if we could we couldn't afford to buy it."

The fourth part of the problem is that, unfortunately, too many families and too many family advisors do not recognize that a valuable piece of land in a family's estate requires special attention and a special kind of estate planning. This could be so for a variety of reasons. Possibly it is not apparent how valuable the land has become. Possibly the land is simply treated as "value" in the estate; if there is an equal amount of "value" of stock in an estate, it may hurt to pay the tax but it is unlikely that selling the stock will lead to teardrops on the family's scrapbook. The standard, even sophisticated estate plan, certainly in Bob and Sue Farmowner's case, often will not protect the family's land. What can Bob and Sue Farmowner do? What can John and Mary Landowner do? What can you do?

Planning for That High Value

As you read through this book, think about the high value in your land. John and Mary don't want to sell Riverview to a developer, but Riverview's development potential, that "extra" value, can create significant problems for their estate. Or, if they plan properly and are smart, they can give away that value, lower their estate taxes, and potentially generate an income tax deduction. The income tax deduction almost seems like a bonus.

The same is true in Bob and Sue's case. Diamond Farm is not worth more than a million dollars as a farm, it is worth more than a million dollars as the beginning of a subdivision. If Bob and Sue can afford to and are willing to forego the very real dollars that could come to them from a cash sale, they can turn that high value into a tax benefit, and preserve the farm for their children.

What Do You Want To Do?

- Is this high value a problem for you? Can it be used to your advantage?
- What are your assets and debts?

- How high is the value of your land compared to the rest of your net worth?

- Is your land likely to appreciate significantly?

- Does your land have development potential?

- Do you have an estate plan? Does the estate plan give special consideration to your real estate?

- Do you know how high the estate tax will be on your estate? See the Landowner's Quiz at Appendix A and the Estate Tax Tables at Appendix B for some help with that question.

- *What do you want to do?*

- Do you want to cash in on the value of your land?

- Do you want to see your land subdivided or turned into a shopping mall?

- Do your children want to see the family land protected?

- Do *you* want to see the family land protected?

- Do you want to keep your land or give it to charity?

The next few chapters will present some of the possibilities for you. The Federal tax laws provide a variety of incentives for land conservation. Those incentives run from keeping your property but imposing restrictions on its future use, to giving away your property to charity at some point in the future, to giving your property to charity immediately.

If you plan right, and take advantage of these incentives, you can accomplish three things. First, you will have protected your land from the developer's bulldozer. Second, you can lower the value of your land for estate tax purposes (or the value of your estate if you give away all or a portion of your land). Third, when you give away that value you are entitled to an income tax deduction that can potentially bring you substantial tax benefits now. With proper planning, by lowering the value of your land and lowering your estate tax burden, it may be possible for your family to avoid selling the land at all.

Some of the Choices
Do you want to keep your land, and protect it?

You may be entitled to an income tax deduction for *protecting your property from development.* That protection takes the form of a recorded restriction on your property, known as a "conservation easement" or a "conservation restriction." *When you create a conservation easement* and donate it to a charitable organization *you still own your land*; the size of the income tax deduction is based on the *value of the development rights you give up.* In addition, since you are reducing the value of your property, the value of your taxable estate drops, your estate tax drops, and your property tax should be lowered. I discuss conservation easements in Chapter 3.

With a conservation easement, you have restricted your right (and the right of any future owner) to develop the land, but you can continue to live on it or farm it, invite guests over or keep trespassers off, or, subject to the restrictions, sell the property, give the property away, or leave the property to your children.

Do you want your land, or a conservation easement, to go to charity, but not until you die?

A second tax incentive for land conservation is a "remainder interest." With a remainder interest, a landowner retains the right to live on his or her land until death, and at death the land goes to the charitable organization. Chapter 4 is on remainder interests.

The gift of a conservation easement or an outright gift of property may be made during the donor's lifetime, and may qualify for an income tax deduction, or the gift may be made in the donor's will. A gift by will is called a "testamentary" gift. If the gift is made in the donor's will, there will be no income tax savings, but the value of the gift will not be included in the donor's estate for estate tax purposes. Gifts by will are discussed in Chapter 5.

Do you want to keep your land in the family but get it out of your estate?

A further possible approach to family land planning and estate planning involves giving your property to other family members while you are alive. A lot of incorrect thinking exists about this subject. In Chapter 6, I briefly review gifts made to family members while you are alive.

Do you want to sell your land now, and cash in on that high value?

Chapter 7 is devoted to a comparison of the rather surprising dollar results if John and Mary sell Riverview to a developer for its maximum development potential or if they put a conservation easement on Riverview but reserve the right to create four more house lots.

What else do you need to know?

Chapters 8 and 9 cover, briefly, some of the other things a landowner will have to do and to keep in mind to get from here to there.

As I mentioned earlier, Appendix B to this book includes Estate Tax Tables that will give you an idea of what the total Federal and state estate tax will be on your estate.

Appendix C includes information on the "alternative minimum tax," or "AMT." Generally, when you make a charitable donation of property that has increased in value since you acquired it, you (or your advisors) may need to know something about the alternative minimum tax. This alternative minimum tax rule was almost repealed in 1992, but today it is still with us. See Appendix C for details.

Appendix D covers a special tax rule that may be helpful to some people who make charitable contributions.

You can't just do nothing.

A generation ago, or even a decade ago, a landowner who cared about his or her land didn't have to do much tax or legal planning, and in many cases didn't have to do any tax or legal planning, to see to it that important family land made it intact to the next generation of owners.

A lot of you who are reading this book *don't like to be told what to do with your real estate.* But listen carefully: if you *don't* take some action, if you *don't* begin planning now, *the government is going to tell your family what to do with your real estate and your heirs aren't going to like what they hear.*

The planning will be different for every landowner and for every family. The planning may well go beyond some of the choices and suggestions in this book. But if you care about your land, and if your land is valuable, and if you want to keep your land intact and pass it to the next generation, you *can't just do nothing.*

Once again, some of the choices.

Once again, some of the choices: a conservation easement, a remainder interest, a gift by will, gifts to other family members while you are alive, a cash sale. Which one is right for John and Mary? Or for Bob and Sue? Or for you?

Let's look first at conservation easements.

CHAPTER 3

Gift of a Conservation Easement

What is a "Conservation Easement"?

Put very simply, a *conservation easement* is a restriction on the use of your property. It is a *recorded deed restriction*, and the *right to enforce the restriction* is given to a tax-exempt charitable organization (generally in the conservation field) or a government agency.

In its most basic form, a conservation easement *will protect* land against future real estate development, industrial use, and many potential commercial uses. A conservation easement generally allows you to *continue current uses*, including, for example, residential and recreational use, agriculture, forestry, or ranching. A conservation easement protects *some important conservation quality* of your land, such as habitat, open space, or scenic views.

Sometimes a "conservation easement" is also referred to as an "easement" or as a *"conservation restriction."* In this book I use the terms interchangeably.

There is more on all of this throughout this book, but this is enough to get you started.

Background

You have the right to do a lot of different things with your property. Subject, of course, to local zoning and public health and safety requirements, a property owner can plant trees or cut them down, build buildings or demolish them, grow crops or raise cattle, grow peonies, dig holes in the property, fence the property in, build a wall around it, and so forth.

The gift of a conservation easement to a charitable organization involves voluntarily giving up *some* of these rights (such as the right to build condos all over the land) and putting in the hands of the new holder of these rights the power to enforce the restrictions on the use of the property. Remember, if you donate an easement you are only limiting *some* of your rights with respect to your property. As I mentioned in Chapter 2, *you continue to own your land*, and you can do anything with your land that is not prevented or restricted by the easement.

Every landowner is unique and every piece of land is unique. Every conservation easement should be unique and must be tailored to meet the needs of *that particular landowner* and *that particular piece of land.*

The "Conservation Purposes" Test

It is important to emphasize that not every easement restricting the future development of property will meet the tax law requirements. The tax law requires that the gift be "for conservation purposes." As a rule, the following generalization works: the more significant the land is, the more it adds to the public good, the more likely it is that you will qualify for the deduction. If you are protecting a large tract of primarily undeveloped property (like John and Mary Landowner) or ranchland or farmland (like Bob and Sue Farmowner), or a smaller parcel of land with scenic or open space qualities, if you are protecting habitat for an important or threatened animal or plant species, if you are preserving a scenic view on a long stretch of roadside that is threatened with subdivision, if you are contributing to a greenbelt around a city or preserving a watershed by a scenic brook or river or lake, your donation is more likely to qualify for a deduction. In addition, you can meet the "conservation purposes" test if you protect important historic property.

You will probably *not* qualify for a deduction if there is nothing special or unusual about the land that you are protecting except that it does not currently have more houses on it. Think of it this way. *If you are truly contributing something to the general environmental well-being of the area, then that's a good (and deductible) gift.* If you are truly trying to get away with something ("maybe I can get a deduction for not permitting any more development on my suburban house lot"), and there is nothing particularly unusual about your property or its setting, you are probably not entitled to an income tax deduction. (As a practical matter, in this latter case, it may be difficult to find a donee organization to accept your easement gift. See Chapter 8.)

If you are in doubt about whether or not an easement on your property would qualify for an income tax deduction, see Chapter 8 for some of the people who can help you answer this question. In many communities around the country, local tax-exempt organizations have been formed precisely for the purpose of protecting open space and other important land in the area. These organizations, often called "land trusts," should be in a good position to assist you.

One final important point about a conservation easement. In many cases it will be possible to qualify for an income tax deduction by giving up the right to develop your property to the maximum possible extent *while still retaining the right to do some limited development in the future.* If a conservation easement preventing any further development on John and Mary Landowner's Riverview would qualify for an income tax deduction, John and Mary could also reserve the right to build, for example, four more houses on Riverview, subject to certain restrictions and limitations, and still qualify for an income tax deduction as long as the property's conservation values continued to be preserved. Remember, however, that in many cases conservation values and *any* further development will be incompatible.

How the Gift is Valued

For purposes of the tax rules, the "value" of a property

is equal to what it would sell for if it were put to the most valuable economic use that is possible under the circumstances. In many cases (though not all), with land that is generally undeveloped or only partially developed, the "value" for estate tax purposes is equal to the highest amount someone would pay for it if it were sold for development.

Let's say that Riverview is worth $2,500,000 to a developer (who would then subdivide the property, build homes on it, and sell homes and/or house lots).

If Riverview were subject to a conservation easement, however, and *could not be subdivided*, the development potential would be non-existent and the value of the property would be considerably lower (although Riverview would still retain some significant value). For example (and remember, this is just an example), let's say the value of Riverview as a 200-acre "estate" that could never be further developed is $1,000,000. For the Landowners' property, then, the value before the easement or restriction would be $2,500,000, and the value after the restriction would be $1,000,000.

Now, here is the rule. In the case of a gift of a conservation easement, *the value of the gift is equal to the difference between the value of the property before the easement and the value of the property after the easement.*

Using the example above, the value of Riverview before the easement or restriction is $2,500,000, the value after the restriction is $1,000,000, and that means *the value of the gift is $1,500,000. That represents the income tax deduction John and Mary are allowed*, subject to limits discussed below.

Consider another possibility for John and Mary. As I suggested earlier, as long as Riverview's conservation values continue to be protected, John and Mary could donate a conservation easement on Riverview and *still retain the right to do some limited development at Riverview in the future*. For example, they could donate a conservation easement on Riverview and reserve the right to build four more houses there, subject to certain restrictions and limitations. In this limited development possibility their house and lot could be worth $900,000 and each of the four "reserved" lots could be worth $150,000. The total value after the restriction would be $1,500,000 ($900,000 plus the four lots at $150,000 each).

In this example, the value of Riverview before the easement is $2,500,000, the value of Riverview after this easement is $1,500,000, so the value of the gift is $1,000,000 ($2,500,000 minus $1,500,000).

For Bob and Sue Farmowner, a conservation restriction on Diamond Farm would likely have a similar, dramatic effect. If Bob and Sue donate an easement that restricts the future use of Diamond Farm to agricultural and/or ranching uses, they will significantly reduce the value of Diamond Farm.

Diamond Farm will now be valued as *farmland* (say that's $1,000 an acre in their area) rather than as a potential subdivision. With Diamond Farm worth $1,500,000 *before* the easement, and $500,000 ($1,000 an acre) *after* the easement, the value of the easement is $1,000,000. Their income tax deduction, then, is $1,000,000. The ability of any family to use these deductions for income tax purposes is limited, as discussed below. But John and Mary have "given away" much or all of that *development value* that was pushing their estate so high, the Farmowners have reduced the value of their estate by $1,000,000, and both families can continue to own, use, and enjoy their family land. If either family at any point does decide to sell, any future owner will be subject to the same restrictions, *and Riverview and Diamond Farm can be saved.*

The Income Tax Deduction

No matter how much any individual gives to charity, limitations in the tax law make it impossible to eliminate the total amount of Federal income tax due.

Let's start with an example.

If John and Mary have annual income of $200,000, even if they make a gift to charity this year of an easement valued at $1,000,000, their tax deduction for the year of the gift *is limited by the tax rules* to $60,000 (30% of their $200,000 income). The "unused" portion of their gift ($940,000) remains available to be "carried forward" and used as a deduction against their income for each of the next five years.

Here is the general rule. A donor can only deduct the value of a gift of land, or of a conservation easement, or of a remainder interest in land (see Chapter 4), up to 30% of the donor's income for the year of the gift. Any amount of the gift remaining after the first year can be carried forward and deducted against income for the following five years.

There is one significant qualification to this rule and there is one significant exception.

First, any gift of "appreciated property" to charity *may* be subject to the "alternative minimum tax." Generally, "appreciated property" is stock, or a painting, or land, for example, that has increased in value since you acquired it. If your gift is subject to the alternative minimum tax, anticipated income tax benefits may be reduced. Again, this alternative minimum tax rule was almost repealed in 1992; see Appendix C for a more extensive discussion of the alternative minimum tax.

Second, in certain circumstances it may be advisable to take advantage of a special rule in the tax law that can potentially help you generate *higher* income tax benefits than those I have discussed above. All the details of the *gift* would be the same, only the tax calculations would change. See Appendix D for a discussion of this special rule.

Finally, note that when the dollar value of the easement gift is significantly higher than the donor's annual income, the 30% limitation may make it impossible to "use up" all of the deduction. In the above illustration, using John and Mary's easement donation valued at $1,000,000, if John and Mary's income remains the same each year, only $360,000 of the gift ($60,000 in the first year and $60,000 for each of the five carryforward years) will be "used up."

The bad news is that the full $1,000,000 value of the gift cannot be used to generate *income tax savings*, because only $360,000 can be deducted under the 30% limitation rule. The good news is that the entire reduction in the value of Riverview is, for John and Mary, an essential step toward *protecting* Riverview, *avoiding* an enormous estate tax bill, and *leaving Riverview to their children.*

Example: John and Mary

John and Mary have a current combined annual income of $200,000 and $40,000 in itemized deductions. They estimate that, not including Riverview, their estate is valued at $2,000,000.

They purchased Riverview, their 200-acre estate, when the area was mostly rural; they paid $100,000. "Suburban sprawl" has made Riverview one of the few remaining local tracts of open space, and that has also made it attractive to developers. Riverview could easily be subdivided and sold off, and the property is now worth $2,500,000.

Working with their advisors (advisors who understand the problems and opportunities and who understand what John and Mary are trying to accomplish; see Chapter 8),

John and Mary donate a conservation easement on River-view to a charitable land conservation organization. In the easement, they reserve the right to keep their house and a large lot and to create (and sell) four additional house lots on Riverview, located in such a manner to protect, to the maximum possible extent, Riverview's important conservation qualities.

Assume that the main house and lot is worth $900,000 and that each of the "reserved" lots is worth $150,000, for a total remaining value of $1,500,000 for Riverview after the easement gift. That gives John and Mary a $1,000,000 charitable contribution.

To make the calculations easy, assume the Landowners' income and deductions are the same for the next five years and that their deductions include $10,000 for state income taxes, $10,000 for property tax, and $20,000 in mortgage interest.

Note in the "Without the Donation" table below, instead of a total of $40,000 in deductions, John and Mary are only allowed $37,157. This is generally because of limitations in the tax law reducing itemized deductions for upper-income individuals and married couples. Later on in this chapter, in Bob and Sue's case, we will see the same limitations do not apply.

Changes in the tax laws currently scheduled to occur in 1996 account for the different tax results in years 5-6 in the tables below. The tables throughout this book do not reflect tax adjustments due to occur in future years based on changes in the cost-of-living index.

Also note that in the "With the Donation" table below, "Deductions" goes from $37,157 without the donation to $97,157 with the donation. This is because of the $60,000 deduction allowable each year (30% of John and Mary's income of $200,000) for the charitable contribution of the easement.

Once again, the facts. (1) John and Mary's income is $200,000. (2) The income tax deduction for the easement is $1,000,000. (3) John and Mary have $40,000 in other itemized deductions. And, once again, see the Appendix for a discussion of the alternative minimum tax, shown as "AMT" in the tables below. As far as the AMT and the tables below are concerned, simply note this: first you calculate the regular tax, *then you calculate the alternative minimum tax, then you pay whichever is higher.*

Without the Donation

	Years 1-4	Years 5-6
Income	$200,000	$200,000
Deductions	37,157	40,000
Tax Due	42,291	40,925

With the Donation

	Year 1	Years 2-4	Years 5-6
Income	$200,000	$200,000	$200,000
Deductions	97,157	97,157	100,000
Regular Tax	23,691	23,691	22,325
AMT	24,000	35,400	35,400
Tax Due	24,000	35,400	35,400

Total tax due over six years *without* the easement donation:
$251,014

Total tax due over six years *with* the easement donation:
$201,000

Income Tax Savings: $50,014

In addition to the income tax savings (reduced because of the AMT but still substantial), John and Mary *have reduced their combined Federal and state estate tax burden* (assuming they live in Massachusetts) from $2,212,900 on a $4,500,000 estate to $1,614,300 on a $3,500,000 estate. In addition, and *this is a very important point*, any or all of the four lots they reserved under the terms of the easement can be sold, at $150,000 each, to help pay the estate tax, and *Riverview can be saved!!*

Good planning? Yes!! In Chapter 7, I discuss this limited development example from another point of view, and the good planning will seem even better.

Example: Bob and Sue

Bob and Sue have a current combined annual income of $40,000. Their estate, not including Diamond Farm, is worth $200,000.

They sign a conservation easement that restricts the future use of Diamond Farm to agricultural and ranching purposes; the value of Diamond Farm is reduced from $1,500,000 to $500,000.

Remember that the charitable contribution can be deducted only up to 30% of Bob and Sue's income. This means that the deduction from the easement will only be $12,000 each year (30% times $40,000). As a result, the *income tax savings from the gift will be low.*

Once again, the facts. (1) Bob and Sue's income is $40,000. (2) The value of the income tax deduction for the easement is $1,000,000. (3) Assume that Bob and Sue have $6,000 in other itemized deductions.

Without the Donation

	Years 1-6
Income	$40,000
Deductions	6,000
Tax Due	4,410

With the Donation

	Years 1-6
Income	$40,000
Deductions	18,000
Regular Tax	2,610
AMT	-0-
Tax Due	2,610

Total tax due over six years *without* the easement donation: $26,460

Total tax due over six years *with* the easement donation: $15,660

Income Tax Savings: $10,800

It is important to note what Bob and Sue have been able to accomplish and what goals they have not yet been able to reach. They have achieved a modest income tax savings and a dramatic reduction in the value of their estate. But they may also want to think about reserving the same sort of *limited development rights* that were so important in John and Mary's case. By retaining the ability to create and sell a small number of lots sensibly located on the perimeter of Diamond Farm, Bob and Sue can create additional liquidity. Lots can be sold now or at a future date. Additional cash will be available to pay any estate tax that may be due. *Diamond Farm can indeed go to the children.*

(This book will not cover special Federal or state estate tax programs designed to assist owners of farms or ranches. You should determine from your advisors whether such programs may be helpful for you.)

Comments and Observations

Let's be absolutely clear about what is motivating John and Mary and Bob and Sue. By restricting Riverview and Diamond Farm, they are protecting their most important asset. By preserving Riverview and Diamond Farm from development, they are also protecting their property, and their families, from the destructive impact of the estate tax.

Some family members, or some family advisors, might argue that John and Mary or Bob and Sue will be giving away a significant portion of their family's wealth. But it is very important to note that aside from achieving important family land protection goals, the "cash" difference to the family is not simply a dollar-for-dollar difference between the value of the property, unrestricted, and the value of the property after giving away the easement.

First of all, a higher-value, unrestricted Riverview or Diamond Farm will generate a *significantly larger estate tax*. Second, any income tax savings as a result of the charitable contribution may provide present dollar benefits and additional *liquid* wealth to the family that chooses to protect its land this way.

Remember: do not be fooled. If you don't *voluntarily* give up some of that high value, *on your own terms* and under a plan that you control, *in the end your family will have to pay much of that value over to Uncle Sam anyway, and on Uncle Sam's terms.*

Comments and Observations–The Alternative Minimum Tax

If the alternative minimum tax rule on charitable gifts is in fact repealed in 1993 or 1994, or ever for that matter, that will be good news for landowners and others who make gifts of appreciated property to charity. With or without the alternative minimum tax, of course, the examples in this chapter and elsewhere in this book will still illustrate the importance of easement donations for John and Mary, for Bob and Sue, and for landowners and families who care about their land.

What If....

Careful tax and conservation planning can create wonderful results for the owners *and* wonderful results for the land. What if John and Mary decide not only that they want Riverview permanently protected but also that they want Riverview to go to a conservation organization when they die?

CHAPTER 4

Gift of a Remainder Interest

Background

A *remainder interest* and a *conservation easement* are two entirely different things.

Today, John and Mary could give the local land trust the deed to Riverview, but could *reserve the right to live at Riverview until they die.* Their right to live at Riverview until they die is called a "life estate" or a "life tenancy." The act of making the gift of Riverview *now*, to *take effect at their deaths,* is called the gift of a "remainder interest."

When you donate an *easement*, you are giving away certain rights you have to do things with your property, but you are not giving up ownership of your property today or in the future and you can sell it or leave it to your children (or to anyone else) at your death. Generally, *when you donate a remainder interest, you have decided to reserve the right to live on your property until your death but your property will go to a charity when you die.*

The first way a remainder interest can qualify for an income tax deduction is by donating to *any* charitable organization a *remainder interest in a personal residence or farm.* This particular donation does not have to meet any of the "conservation purposes" tests, discussed in Chapter 3, that are important for *easement* donations. A common form that this gift takes, for example, is for a donor to give his *alma mater* a remainder interest in the donor's home. The donor continues to live on the property, and, at the donor's death, the *alma mater* sells the home and uses the proceeds in the conduct of its educational business. The simple gift of a remainder interest in a personal residence to a conservation organization or to any other charity, *without any restrictions on the future use of the property,* could qualify for an income tax deduction.

However, if John and Mary are motivated by a desire to protect Riverview, they should consider the second form of a gift of a remainder interest, the gift of a remainder interest in land "for conservation purposes." Again, this is the same "conservation purposes" test that applies to the deductible donation of conservation easements, discussed in Chapter 3. Remember that to meet the conservation purposes test the contribution must truly add to the public conservation good: preservation of important open space, significant wildlife habitat, threatened farmland or watershed, protection of historic property, and so forth. In the case of property that is the subject of a remainder gift for conservation purposes, during the landowner's "life estate" or "life tenancy" the landowner will not be able to do anything with that property that will destroy the conservation qualities to be protected by the gift.

How the Gift is Valued

If John and Mary give their children $1,000,000 today, the value of that gift is clearly $1,000,000. But what if John and Mary put that same $1,000,000 in a trust, and the terms of that trust say that John and Mary's children can't have that $1,000,000 for ten years? The *value* of the right to receive $1,000,000 in ten years is certainly less than the *value* of the right to receive $1,000,000 today.

Similarly, John and Mary can give Riverview to a charitable conservation organization *today*. The value of that gift is much greater than if John and Mary agree *now* to give Riverview to the local land trust *when they die*.

With the gift of a remainder interest, the fact that the donee organization will actually take possession of the property at some time in the future results in the value of the gift being reduced *for income tax deduction purposes*.

Let's say that John and Mary reserve the right to live at Riverview until they both die ("life estates"), and today sign a deed by which Riverview will go to the local land trust after their deaths (the gift of a "remainder interest"). Let's assume that John and Mary own Riverview jointly, that John is 65 and Mary is 62, and that Riverview is worth $2,500,000.

Based on recent IRS tables, the value of the remainder interest is $889,400. (According to the IRS tables, the "factor" to be used in this particular case is .35576; the value of Riverview, $2,500,000, is multiplied by the factor of .35576 to get the result of $889,400.)

As another example, if John Landowner is widowed and 65 years old, and John donates to a local conservation organization a remainder interest in Riverview for conservation purposes, the factor from the IRS tables is .39656. The value of the deduction is $991,400 (.39656 times $2,500,000).

The IRS factor has *nothing to do* with the current value of Riverview. In the previous example, if Riverview were worth $500,000 instead of $2,500,000, the factor would still be .39656 and the value of the deduction would be $198,280 (.39656 times $500,000).

As with the gift of a conservation easement or an outright gift of land, the value of the remainder interest is generally only deductible up to 30% of the donor's income, with a five-year carryforward of the balance of the deduction.

There is a Better Way

I suggest that John and Mary are missing the boat. We start with the proposition that Riverview has the characteristics (open space, scenic view, whatever) that would satisfy the "conservation purposes" test, and that John and Mary want Riverview protected. We add to that the fact that once the conservation remainder has been donated, neither John nor Mary nor any other owner of Riverview can do anything on or to Riverview that is inconsistent with the conservation gift.

Now we have an opportunity to use two different con-

servation and tax tools together, with good results!!

I suggest that if John and Mary care about Riverview and wish to reduce their taxes they should give both a conservation easement on Riverview and a conservation remainder. They will be giving up nothing more than if the conservation remainder donation were the only gift, and the tax benefits will be considerably greater. For purposes of both the tax law and enforcement of the restrictions, I generally recommend that the easement go to one conservation organization and the remainder go to a different conservation organization. The gifts can be made at the same time or in the same year or the easement can be given in one year and the remainder interest can be given in a later year (for technical legal reasons, you may want to donate the easement first). It may even be possible to make both gifts at the same time using only one document.

Compare the tax benefits.

John Landowner is widowed and 65 years old. He gives to a charitable conservation organization an easement on Riverview, prohibiting any further development, and reduces the value of Riverview from $2,500,000 to $1,000,000. His income tax deduction is $1,500,000.

In the same year, he gives a remainder interest in Riverview (which is now restricted by the conservation easement) to a second conservation organization. The discount factor is .39656; the value of Riverview *at the time of this donation* (reduced by the easement) is $1,000,000. The income tax deduction from the remainder donation is $396,560 (.39656 times $1,000,000). The total income tax deduction is $1,896,560, compared to $991,400 with only the donation of the remainder interest. John has not really given up anything additional, since his use of Riverview is subject to the same conservation restrictions in both cases. He has just been smarter about his tax planning.

Remember, of course, as I noted in Chapter 3, *a larger income tax deduction will not always mean larger income tax savings*, because the value of the gift can generally only be deducted up to 30% of the donor's income. Obviously, each donor must review the possible results with his or her tax advisor.

Finally, keep in mind that the gift of a remainder interest, whether for conservation purposes or not and just like any other charitable contribution of appreciated property, may be subject to the alternative minimum tax.

A Warning

One further warning for conservation-minded landowners who plan to give away their property, either in the form of a remainder donation or in an outright gift. *If you want your land to be protected, before you give it away put a conservation easement on it and donate that easement to a conservation organization.*

The horror stories often go like this. Grandpa had an informal understanding with his favorite college that the college would preserve his old mansion and its beautiful gardens and use the place as an administration building. In his will, he left them the property outright, with no restrictions on its future use. Five years after Grandpa died, the college tore down the old mansion, citing pressing needs for space, and now faculty housing covers the flowerbeds. The family can do nothing.

Grandpa *could have* mixed and matched conservation giving and other charitable giving. A conservation easement donated to a charitable conservation organization would have protected the old homestead, and the property still could have been left to the college. If the college needed cash, the property could have been sold, *subject to the restrictions*, to any buyer who was willing to use the property in accordance with the terms of Grandpa's easement.

What If....

What if John and Mary don't want to get involved with all of these legal documents now? Can they simply make a gift to charity of an easement, or of Riverview, in their wills?

CHAPTER 5

A Testamentary Gift (Gift by Will)

Mother Had the Last Word

I heard a story not too long ago that may or may not be true. An elderly woman on Cape Cod, it seems, owned more than 50 acres of open and scenic property. She had summered in the big home there when she was a child and subsequently inherited the property from her parents. She had a deep love for the land and wanted to see it preserved.

Her children liked what they heard from local developers, who coveted the property and made a number of offers to the elderly owner, all of which she turned down.

Finally, her children thought they won the battle. Mother had wanted to put a conservation restriction on the property, but she agreed that she would not do so during her lifetime. The children expected that when she died, they could cash in on the property's enormous value.

The children were wrong. Mother donated a conservation restriction on the property to the local land conservation organization, but she made the donation *in her will.*

You Can Make a Gift by Will

A charitable contribution of a conservation easement or an outright gift of property can be made, just like any other testamentary bequest, by will. For estate tax purposes, the full value of the gift is included in the estate and then deducted from the estate. As a *tax* matter, it is as if the property had been restricted or given away before death (and kept out of the estate at the outset). Please note, however, that any sizable charitable contribution by will *could* have other effects (in connection with the division of property under the will or the funding of certain trusts), and a careful analysis of this matter should be made for you ahead of time by an experienced estate-tax counselor.

In addition, if you plan to make a conservation gift by will you should certainly ascertain ahead of time that the named charity will accept the gift. One way to avoid this problem (and a host of other problems that may come up in carrying out your wishes) in the case of a testamentary gift of an easement is to *include in your will specific and detailed language imposing a conservation easement, worked out with the charitable organization, to take effect at your death.*

There are advantages and disadvantages to making charitable conservation gifts by will. *Unlike a lifetime gift, which for income tax purposes is generally subject to a deduction ceiling of 30% of income, a gift by will is fully deductible for estate tax purposes. Further, the alternative*

*minimum tax does not apply to gifts of appreciated property
made by will.*

*On the other hand, of course, if you make a gift by will
you do not get an income tax deduction and, of course, you
cannot take advantage of any income tax savings.*

You May Want to do More Than That

Unless you are planning to handle the problem like the
woman at the Cape, and if you are certain that you want to
protect your land by making a conservation gift, you have a
great deal to gain by making that gift while you are alive,
and making the most out of any income tax deductions,
rather than making a gift by will. Obviously, if you are not
certain about what you want to do, revising your will to include a conservation gift (either an easement or an outright
gift of the property) can give you estate tax "protection"
while at the same time preserving your right to change your
mind. Comprehensive planning can also include gifts at
death through the use of trusts created during the donor's
lifetime; this is often a flexible and desirable technique and
you should discuss it with your advisors.

A landowner who fully intends to leave land outright to
a conservation organization at his or her death should remember that the current gift of a remainder interest to a
charitable organization will generate income tax deductions
that will produce tax savings. Further, as I indicated in Chapter 4 on remainder interests, once you have decided to donate a remainder interest for conservation purposes there is

another important step you can take. You can possibly create further tax benefits without giving up any additional rights by donating an easement on the property before you donate the remainder interest.

What If....

What if John and Mary aren't so charitably inclined this year, but are still sensitive to the estate tax burden Riverview will generate? Can't they just give the property to their children?

CHAPTER 6

Giving to Other Family Members Now

It Won't Work This Way

"Why should I worry about the estate tax?" John Land-owner asks. "We'll just sign the property over to the children, and Mary and I will stay here as long as we want."

This is something that I hear from time to time and every time I do it makes me cringe.

This is not as simple or as painless as it sounds. Not only that, "signing the property over to the children" may give John and Mary a false sense of security, and as a result they may not take *similar* tax-planning steps that *do work.*

The Rules

In order to know what is wrong with John and Mary's idea, there are a few tax rules we need to understand about gifts to other family members while you are alive (sometimes called "lifetime giving").

First, if you give away property to someone other than your spouse, but *retain the right to use or enjoy that property, the value of the property (the property you thought you had given away) will be included in your estate at your death.* It is important to recognize the significance of this rule. If John and Mary "give away" Riverview, for example, to their children, but if they continue to live at Riverview and use the property and enjoy it, the full value of Riverview will be included in their estates when they die.

Why is this so? In part, this is because the tax law takes the position that if John and Mary retain the right to continue to use and enjoy Riverview, they truly haven't given Riverview away. In fact, the IRS would argue, the only reason John and Mary signed Riverview over to the children was to try to avoid the estate tax.

Now, note that if John and Mary signed Riverview over to the children and moved into a place in town, the results would be quite different. Under those circumstances, the value of Riverview would not be included in their estates when they die. But the gift of Riverview to the children now would be a *taxable gift.*

"What!?" you say. "Do you mean that if I just deed my house over to my children and move out I have to pay a tax?"

The answer is, it depends (that sounds just like a lawyer). *The second tax rule that is important for this chapter* is that you can generally give away up to $10,000 a year ($20,000 if spouses join in the gift; check with your advisor for details) to as many different people as you would like without any gift tax liability. If you want to give away property *faster* than that, *you may have to pay a gift tax.* Whether or not John and Mary will actually have to pay a gift tax on the gift of Riverview to the children will depend, among other things, on how much Riverview is worth and on whether or not they have made other gifts, this year or in prior years, above the $10,000 per person ceiling.

The third tax rule that is important for this chapter is that spouses can make unlimited gifts to each other, while they are alive or at death (by will), without any Federal gift tax or estate tax. Cash, stocks, land, anything, it generally doesn't matter for Federal gift tax or estate tax purposes as long as the transfer is from one spouse to another.

The fourth tax rule that is important for this chapter is this. In addition to allowing individuals to make annual $10,000 gifts (again, $20,000 if spouses give together), and in addition to allowing spouses to make unlimited gifts to each other, the Federal tax law generally allows each individual to transfer to others $600,000 of property (cash, stocks, land, *any* property), during lifetime or at death, without paying any Federal estate tax or gift tax. (There have been rumblings in Congress in recent years to reduce this $600,000 amount to a lower number so as to *increase estate taxes*. This would be a *terrible result* for landowners and would make planning for landowners who care about their land much more difficult.)

What does all this mean? *If you want to give valuable property to your family while you are alive, before you do you must consult a tax attorney.*

Done Right, Lifetime Giving Might Make Sense

Giving Riverview to the children now, even if John and Mary have to pay a gift tax, may turn out to be a smart thing to do.

For example, if Riverview is worth $500,000 now and increases in value at a rate of 7% a year, in 10 years the value of Riverview will have almost doubled. The property will then be a million-dollar asset for John and Mary to contend with in their estates. On the other hand, if John and Mary give Riverview to their children now (of course, assuming that they can afford to and assuming that it otherwise makes good sense), the future increase in value of Riverview will not be taxed as part of their estates.

There are other lifetime giving techniques that John and Mary should consider.

For example, if Riverview is worth $500,000, and if John and Mary have two married children, they can give each child and each child's spouse $20,000 "worth" of Riverview each year. The best way to set up this sort of family giving program will vary from family to family and from state to state. Your professional advisor will be able to help you on this point. In five years, they would be able to give away $400,000 of the "value" of Riverview (although if Riverview continues to appreciate, it may take longer than John and Mary think to give away all of Riverview this way). One potential risk that John and Mary run, of course, is that if the long-term preservation of Riverview is important to them, without careful planning this annual giving may be wonderful for estate tax purposes but the children (bless them) may one day sell out or divorce. This leads to a further planning possibility. John and Mary could put a conservation restriction on Riverview, reducing its value, generating an income tax deduction, and permanently protecting it. Then John and Mary could begin a program of annual family gifts, in the end giving away Riverview in a shorter period of time.

If John and Mary have enough other assets and are the kind of people who for tax and family reasons make annual gifts to their children and possibly their grandchildren, giving the family Riverview may be preferable to giving the family cash. As I noted earlier, if Riverview continues to appreciate, getting it (and the potential future appreciation) out of their estates early may be a sensible thing to do.

Other Techniques

There are a variety of other, more specialized wealth-transfer techniques, including the use of trusts that can run for many generations, life insurance, and charitable trusts, that I have not covered here. Further, the estate tax consequences of any family gift program should be thoroughly reviewed in light of relatively recent Federal estate tax valuation rules. Once again, however, this book is only designed to provide an introduction to some of the tax issues and techniques involved in family land preservation. A good advisor should be able to provide you with a more extensive menu, and can help you integrate estate-planning techniques with current family needs.

CHAPTER 7

Cash Sale Compared to Limited Development

Thanks, But We'll Take The Cash

"We're glad you have taken the time to share this all with us," John and Mary might now say. "But we think we'll take the money."

What does the Landowner family end up with if John and Mary sell Riverview now, while prices are high? *Much less than they think.*

If the sale price is $2,500,000, and the cost of Riverview was $100,000, they have $2,400,000 of gain; the Federal income tax on the gain is $665,666 (without taking into consideration any special Federal income tax benefits that might be available to John and Mary on the sale of their principal residence). Assume John and Mary live in Massachusetts; the Massachusetts tax on the gain is $144,000. John and Mary now take the after-tax proceeds of the sale, $1,690,334, and invest that money in tax-free municipals. (For these calculations we will not include any income on the municipals.)

Mary dies first, leaving everything to John. When John dies, assume he leaves $2 million in other assets, and the municipals, to the children:

- The Federal estate tax on the $3,690,334 estate is $1,229,489. The Massachusetts estate tax is $499,050. Total tax due? $1,728,539!!! (See the Estate Tax Tables at Appendix B. Note also that the Massachusetts estate tax is scheduled to be somewhat reduced over the next few years.)

- *The proceeds from the sale of Riverview are almost gone.* Outrageous? Confiscatory? Poor planning? True!!

- *Riverview is gone.* Eighty houses and a small park cover the once-loved site.

- After paying estate taxes, the Landowner family has $1,961,795 left.

Is This a Better Idea?

Now, compare this awful result with the limited development possibility we discussed in Chapter 3. Remember that John and Mary put a conservation easement on Riverview but reserved the right to keep their house and large lot and to create four additional house lots on Riverview. The value of Riverview was reduced to $1,500,000; the deduction was $1,000,000; the income tax savings from the easement donation was $50,014.

Assume the Landowners hold Riverview until they die. The estate of the survivor, consisting of $2,000,000 plus Riverview (to keep it simple we will assume no increase in the value of Riverview), is taxed as follows:

- The Federal estate tax on the $3,500,000 estate is $1,143,800. The Massachusetts estate tax is $470,500.

- The four "reserved" lots on Riverview can be sold, at $150,000 each, to help pay the estate tax. Because the Landowners held their land until they died, there will be no (or very little) tax to pay on the proceeds of these sales. (See below for an explanation of this point.)

- If John and Mary's heirs don't want to keep Riverview, it can be sold (again, with little or no tax to pay), but *Riverview will forever be protected.*

- After paying estate taxes, the Landowner family has $1,885,700 left, *including Riverview.* If we add to that the $50,014 income tax savings from the easement donation, *the dollar difference between selling out and holding on has virtually disappeared and John and Mary have left more value to their children by preserving Riverview.*

- Good planning? True!!

The same limited development possibilities also work well for the family that has current cash needs. Under such circumstances, John and Mary could consider the possibility of protecting Riverview with a conservation easement reserving limited development rights, and then selling one or more lots. With proper planning, the charitable contribution deduction can be used against a portion of the gain from the sale of the lots. Your advisors can help you with this planning.

As I mentioned above, because John and Mary held Riverview until they died, if the house lots are sold shortly after their deaths there will be little or no tax to pay on the proceeds of the sales. This is because of an important tax rule. When an individual dies owning property (stocks, land, *any* kind of property), the "basis" (generally speaking, the *cost*) of that property is increased (or "stepped up") *for income tax purposes* to whatever the *value* of that property was at the death of the owner. In other words, in the above example, if the *value* of each of the reserved lots was $150,000 after the deaths of John and Mary, and those lots were subsequently sold for $150,000 each, there would be *no gain for income tax purposes*, which means, of course, that no income tax would be due because of the sale.

For many property owners the *dollar* comparison between selling and preserving (with limited development) will not be as close as it is in John and Mary's case, above. But the point is clear. You do have choices.

Is There a Message Here?

Yes!!

Don't assume that any particular plan or approach will produce the best after-tax dollar results. Run the numbers!!

What's Next?

A general understanding of how to use the various tax incentives for land conservation to generate income tax savings and estate tax savings is only one piece of the family land planning puzzle. Who else should the Farmowners talk to? What else do the Landowners need to know to start?

CHAPTER 8

Sources of Help, And Other Issues

What Do I Give Up? And What Do I Keep?

Being able to figure out the income tax and estate tax benefits from a gift of land or a conservation easement may be remarkably easy compared to being able to reach agreement among family members about what (if anything) should be done with the family's land (if in fact the owner or owners of the land seek input from other family members).

For some families, the land may be their single most valuable asset; reducing or restricting its value may simply be unaffordable. In other families, significant land with important conservation qualities may be only a small piece of wealth compared to other family assets, but inertia may outweigh social conscience and financial planning and the land will go on the auction block.

Then there are those families willing to forego some value (even if it hurts a little) for the sake of preserving an irreplaceable asset. For these people, agreement on a family land conservation plan that takes into consideration current and future financial and conservation goals may be easy to arrive at or it may be the product of extensive debates and even loud arguments.

It will be helpful for these people to know that, in most cases, once a landowner has made the choice to preserve his or her property, there may be a range of ways to do that. For example, as Chapter 7 illustrates, with a property of any considerable size, the ability to do some additional limited development while preserving *almost* all of the property's conservation values may provide the necessary flexibility to protect the property while still retaining much of its dollar value.

In addition, the state of the art of land planning and tax and legal planning for landowners is becoming better each year. With the help of a knowledgeable advisor who can provide the family with a wide range of choices, the family that is willing to work together can almost always resolve a "preserve it/sell it" dispute. If you are in the middle of such a dispute, or if you think you might be when some of your family members find out you are reading this book, the "resource people" identified below should be able to help you sort out and evaluate the various options that may be available to you.

Recipient of the Gift

For the gift to be eligible for an income tax deduction, a charitable conservation organization or a unit of government must agree to hold the easement (or the property). In some limited situations, a charity that is not primarily conservation-oriented may be an eligible donee for a conservation easement, but this is the exception rather than the rule. Obviously, at some early point in their planning the Landowners will have to identify a donee for their gift.

Many land trusts around the country have well-informed staff or volunteers who can provide invaluable technical assistance and advice to a potential donor, including names of land planning, legal, and other professional advisors who may be an integral part of the process. Many land conservation organizations will also have literature that will be helpful to you in your planning.

If you don't know where to begin asking about a donee organization, you can start anywhere from a local land trust to a local conservation commission to a State Game and Fish Department (throughout this book, references to "conservation organizations" mean both private charitable organizations and state or local governmental conservation agencies). If there is one in your area, a local land trust will most certainly give you a warm welcome.

Some national conservation organizations, such as The Nature Conservancy, the Trust for Public Land, the National Audubon Society, or the American Farmland Trust, have regional or even state offices. The staff people will be very knowledgeable about who in your particular area might be a logical choice as a donee.

The Land Trust Alliance, with a national office at 900 Seventeenth Street, N.W., Washington, DC 20006 (202-785-1410), can help you identify local land trusts and other conservation organizations and can also provide you with background literature. A Land Trust Alliance publication, "The Conservation Easement Handbook" (a joint project with the Trust for Public Land), includes much useful material. Another Land Trust Alliance publication, "Appraising Easements" (a joint project with the National Trust for Historic Preservation), should be helpful for your appraiser.

Legal Advice, Including Tax

The donation of land to charity should not be done without the advice of an attorney who is experienced in this specialty or willing to affiliate with someone who is. An outright gift of land is generally a simple matter; the gift of a conservation easement or remainder interest is not; and all of these gifts involve significant tax consequences.

"Of course he's going to say that," you think. "He's a tax lawyer." *Anyone who tells you this task can be undertaken without competent tax and other legal advice doesn't understand the seriousness of what is being accomplished.* If you give away your property, it's gone, forever. If you record a conservation easement on your property, you have not only forever restricted your ability to do with it what you please, you have also given some outside organization the authority to enforce those restrictions. Now, in many cases these are truly fine and wonderful things to do, but if you do them you should do them right.

Your lawyer should do them right, too. If you find a lawyer to do this work for you, *ask the lawyer how many times he or she has done this sort of thing before.* If you don't know where to turn, local land conservation organizations ought to be able to help you find good, experienced legal help; your donee organization may be a good place to start.

Remember that in addition to understanding the law of conservation easements, *your tax advisor must also be sensitive to all the related tax and legal planning that should be done in connection with your gift.*

This book does *not* consider the tax consequences of a bargain sale. In a bargain sale, the owner *sells* an asset to a charitable organization for less than its current value; the sale generates for the seller *both* taxable gain and a charitable contribution deduction. Many tax-exempt charitable organizations do not have sufficient funds to participate in a bargain sale. If the charity you identify can pay you, your advisors should be able to help you determine the tax consequences.

The cost of legal advice will vary with the complexity of the donation. In the case of an outright gift of property, the fee for preparing a deed usually will be nominal if no subdivision is involved. In a simple easement case, with one donor and very limited reserved rights, the fee for drafting a conservation easement should be *relatively* low. The legal costs begin to grow as more parties become involved and, for example, as the landowner and his or her lawyer begin to negotiate with the charity over the extent of the reserved rights. In addition, costs go up when the landowner wants the lawyer to do most of the negotiating.

As a general rule, in a *very simple case* the legal fees for a conservation easement could be $2,500 or less, not including any possible fees for travel time. Depending on the complexity of the work the cost could be significantly higher. In one case I am aware of, several family members had the opportunity to review, disagree about, and comment on numerous drafts of an easement, and the legal fees were well in excess of $20,000.

For many landowners and many families, a conservation easement is only one part of a larger family land planning, estate planning, and asset planning project. *Do not be "penny wise and pound foolish." Comprehensive and successful planning is not inexpensive, but comprehensive and successful planning for families that own land is an important and intelligent investment for current and future generations.*

Appraiser

You must hire an appraiser.

Under the tax law, any person who makes a charitable contribution of property with a claimed value in excess of $5,000 must have a "qualified appraisal" or the tax deduction for the gift will be disallowed.

A "qualified appraisal" must include, among other things, a description of the property, the method used to determine its value, information about the appraiser's qualifications, and a description of the fee arrangement between the donor and the appraiser.

Once again, in addition to the practical requirement that an appraiser be hired, the earlier a donor has an idea of what the value of the contribution will be, the more opportunity will exist for any tax planning that might be advisable in the year of the gift. For a donor who is considering reserving some future development rights, an early valuation review of the different possibilities is a good idea.

The cost of an appraisal may run from $500 for the simplest house appraisal to $10,000 for a complex appraisal of an easement with significant reserved rights.

The value of a good appraisal cannot be emphasized too much: in an audit with the IRS, the qualifications of the appraiser and the thoroughness of the appraisal can be very important factors.

Land Planner or Consultant

A land planner or consultant can help you review different limited development possibilities for your land.

There are a number of situations in which such an advisor will *not* be necessary. A donor who is not going to reserve any future development rights will not need a land planner. A donor with a very large tract of land who wants to reserve the right to carve out a few house lots *may* not require such services. Additionally, the need for the preparation and even possible recording of a plan preserving future development rights will vary widely from state to state.

Your legal advisor can help you determine whether a land planner is necessary.

In some situations, as I noted in Chapter 3, *any* further development will simply be incompatible with conservation goals. Also, in some situations the reservation of too many future development rights may also threaten a landowner's claim to an income tax deduction for the donation of a conservation easement. In other situations, however, it may be possible, through sensitive siting and with a minimum of intrusion, to do limited future building on restricted property.

A land planner who is sensitive both to environmental and open space concerns and to the tax law's requirements for the deductibility of an easement donation can help. Such planners can often bring to a project not just sensitive and practical planning techniques but also appraisal capabilities.

If you need such a person, the same sources of information referred to above (land trusts and other charitable conservation organizations, etc.) should be able to point you in the right direction. Make sure you have some confirmation that any person you retain has done this sort of work before.

The cost of a land planner or consultant will generally run from $5,000 to $20,000, depending on the size of your parcel, the number of limited development options to be considered, and the complexity of the situation. This is a fair price to pay for proper management of an illiquid asset. In fact, a fee in this range for a comprehensive review of development/conservation options on a $2,000,000 piece of property compares favorably with the usual fees for proper management of a comparably-valued securities portfolio, especially when you consider that a sensible limited development plan, when implemented, will often result in major income and estate tax savings.

Surveyor

You may need a survey to clarify the boundaries of your property. Sometimes the donee organization, such as a land trust, may require a current survey. Ask your legal advisor or consultant what the price range should be in your state for a survey of your property. Keep two things in mind. First, survey work need only be done after you have made the final decision about what to do with your land. Second, it may take months to secure the services of a qualified surveyor and to have the job completed.

Deductibility

Many of the costs and fees discussed above are deductible in figuring your Federal income tax to the extent they exceed, when added to certain other miscellaneous itemized deductions, 2% of your adjusted gross income. Note that this is *not* the same as the deduction for the charitable contribution itself. Check with your advisor for details.

Property Taxes

The gift of a conservation restriction on land will reduce the value of that land, often considerably. If you donate a conservation restriction on your property, it would stand to reason that your property tax should drop. Unfortunately, I understand that many local assessors are not immediately responsive to the drop in value of restricted property, and some conservation-minded donors may end up fighting city hall over this matter.

Your attorney will be able to help you with the planning on this issue, should that become necessary. There are court decisions that state that when the value of property is reduced by a conservation restriction, the property tax assessment should generally drop to reflect the restrictions.

In addition, many states and municipalities have special assessment programs for property where the use is restricted to farmland or open space. Your advisors can help you determine whether your property is eligible for any of these programs.

Timing

One particular lesson I have learned through the course of my work in this field is that it always takes longer than expected to do all the necessary work and complete the gift of a conservation restriction. If a landowner wants to complete a conservation gift in a particular year, tax planning and planning for the gift should begin *as early in the year as possible.* In some cases, the work can be done quickly, but a donor should not count on that happening. Sometimes when a survey is required it turns out that no qualified local surveyor can *begin* the work for months, let alone deliver a finished product in time.

If different generations within a family are asked to participate, the planning process can be a lengthy one. Giving away land or restricting its use means giving up wealth, and no matter what the social (or even the tax) benefits, some family members may be opposed. Difficult non-tax issues often come up when many family members own (or expect to own) the same land together; guidance from an experienced legal advisor and early planning are essential in these situations.

A successful compromise, if one can be reached, will often involve keeping some significant value, and potential liquidity, by reserving limited development rights. With a large tract of land the variations on this theme can be endless. The message is simple: allow adequate time for planning.

Comments and Observations

The charitable gift of land or of a conservation easement can involve a lot of work, a lot of planning (much of which your advisors can do for you), possibly a lot of decisions, and some expense. In many cases, the income tax savings from the charitable deduction can help "recover" much of the out-of-pocket expense, and this certainly underscores the value of good tax planning. However, in a much broader sense, for the landowners with whom I have worked, the deep satisfaction of permanently preserving their own land far outweighs any of the short-term work and costs.

CHAPTER 9

What Do I Do Now?

You know now (in fact, you knew before you opened this book) that you want to do something to protect your land. You may have discussed this matter with your family. You are ready to move ahead. But you need more information and you need more help.

Where is the Best Place to Start?

If you ask a person from a local land conservation organization where to begin, he or she is likely to say, "Start with us. We can help you through the decision-making process and we can identify other good resource people and professionals if you need them."

If you ask a land planning consultant with experience in this specialty where to begin the answer will probably be, "Start with me. I know what I need to know to get you through the process. I can coordinate everything."

An attorney who has done land conservation work would reply to your question, "Let's begin now. I can provide you with a checklist of the things you need to do and we can talk about the decisions you have to make."

Who is right? They all are. This is a narrow enough area of life and law so that once you step inside it and make the decision to go ahead, any of these specialists can help you begin to put things together.

Please note this, however. *We are talking about a specialized area of family and financial planning.* You should not ask a brilliant personal injury lawyer to handle the probate of your mother's estate and you should not ask a tax lawyer to defend a client against a drunken driving charge. Similarly, it is a rare family counselor who knows how to solve the family's land planning problems and complete the family's land planning project. *If necessary, a specialist should be retained to work with the family's lawyer on this particular matter.*

If you still don't know where to begin, find a city or town official who is knowledgeable about land conservation and environmental protection and get a few names of qualified professionals or state or local charitable land trusts or other conservation organizations. One or two telephone calls should put you in touch with the right person or people. If the person you are talking to does not understand what you want to do, you have not yet found the right person. You will know when you have found the right people because *they will understand exactly what you are talking about* and they will be very glad to hear from you.

Your desire to protect and preserve your land and to confront your estate-tax problem has taken you this far. Re-read Chapter 1 and remember, *doing nothing about your land can have awful consequences.* So don't stop now, and good luck.

Stephen J. Small
Boston, Massachusetts
November, 1992

APPENDIX A

The Landowner's Quiz

What do you think the combined Federal and state estate tax would be on your estate? Fill in the information below.

1. My net worth, *not including* the value of my real estate, is:

2. The value of my real estate is:

3. Therefore, the total value of my estate is:

4. If my estate were fully taxable, the combined Federal and state estate tax would be:

5. In order to pay this tax, my heirs will have to:

**DON'T LOOK AT THE ESTATE TAX TABLES IN
APPENDIX B UNTIL YOU HAVE COMPLETED THIS PAGE**

Estate Tax Tables

Total Federal and State Estate Tax Due at Death

Comments and Observations

The Estate Tax Tables that follow show the different levels of estate tax due, in all 50 states and the District of Columbia, based on rates and information available in late 1992.

Under the laws of some states, there may be variations that could change the results in the tables. To keep the tables as simple as possible, I have assumed that those variations do not apply. *You must check with your advisor to determine how the estate tax rules in your own state will affect your own particular situation and your family's situation.* Some states, for example, have an *inheritance* tax instead of an estate tax. The *effect* is the same: the total dollar amount due, shown in the tables, must be paid to the Federal and state government.

In addition, as with Federal and state *income* tax rates and rules, Federal and state *estate* tax rates and rules can change. For example, the *Massachusetts* estate tax rates are scheduled to change in 1993 and future years. In some states, *gift taxes* are significant. *Check with your advisor about the rates and rules in your own state.* (Note that even with some variations from state to state, the overall results are fairly close among almost all states.)

All this having been said, however, the tables make absolutely clear the *enormous impact* of estate taxes. Note that in many states (such as Florida, for example) popularly thought to be "havens" from high estate taxes, significant Federal and state estate taxes can be due once the taxable estate exceeds $600,000. On a $2,000,000 taxable estate, *in every state, no less than $588,000 is due in taxes.* On a $2,500,000 taxable estate, *in every state, no less than $833,000 is due in taxes.* On a $5,000,000 taxable estate, in every state, *no less than $2,198,000 is due in taxes.*

* **"Most States"** column on the next page includes tax for Alabama, Alaska, Arizona, Arkansas, California, Colorado, District of Columbia, Florida, Georgia, Hawaii, Idaho, Illinois, Maine, Minnesota, Mississippi, Missouri, Montana, Nevada, New Hampshire, New Jersey, New Mexico, North Dakota, Oregon, Rhode Island, South Carolina, Texas, Utah, Vermont, Virginia, Washington, West Virginia, Wisconsin, Wyoming

Total Federal and State Estate Tax Due in Every State on Taxable Estates of Various Dollar Amounts

Amount of Your Taxable Estate:	$600,000	$1,000,000	$2,000,000	$2,500,000	$5,000,000	$10,000,000
Estate Tax Due by State:						
*Most States	0	153,000	588,000	833,000	2,198,000	4,948,000
Connecticut	37,895	197,735	680,735	943,735	2,341,935	4,987,935
Delaware	31,250	175,050	603,650	839,450	2,198,000	4,948,000
Indiana	24,950	171,700	630,150	885,950	2,248,150	4,948,000
Iowa	39,825	182,041	601,153	833,000	2,198,000	4,948,000
Kansas	21,750	155,560	588,000	833,000	2,198,000	4,948,000
Kentucky	45,350	193,170	624,910	860,130	2,198,000	4,948,000
Louisiana	17,050	153,000	588,000	833,000	2,198,000	4,948,000
Maryland	6,000	153,000	588,000	833,000	2,198,000	4,948,000

Total Federal and State Estate Tax Due in Every State on Taxable Estates of Various Dollar Amounts
(continued)

Amount of Your Taxable Estate:	$600,000	$1,000,000	$2,000,000	$2,500,000	$5,000,000	$10,000,000
Estate Tax Due by State:						
Massachusetts	55,500	225,300	733,900	1,014,700	2,511,900	5,385,900
Michigan	34,472	191,457	660,557	916,607	2,280,057	4,948,000
Nebraska	5,900	153,000	588,000	833,000	2,198,000	4,948,000
New York	25,500	173,300	634,900	894,700	2,347,900	5,316,900
North Carolina	7,000	154,800	608,400	864,200	2,271,400	4,948,000
Ohio	30,100	177,900	616,500	857,300	2,198,000	4,948,000
Oklahoma	17,725	165,525	613,250	859,050	2,198,000	4,948,000
Pennsylvania	36,000	179,800	608,400	844,200	2,198,000	4,948,000
South Dakota	41,250	191,050	634,650	877,950	2,198,000	4,948,000
Tennessee	0	153,000	609,800	863,100	2,212,800	4,948,000

APPENDIX C

The Alternative Minimum Tax – Here Today, Gone Tomorrow?

A Quick Look

There is no such thing as a "quick look" at the alternative minimum tax.

It is important for landowners at least to understand that the AMT may be involved in determining the tax savings from a charitable contribution, and some readers may be interested in wading through this highly technical material. However, you must rely on a professional advisor to do the AMT calculations for your own particular case.

Background

For many years, the Treasury Department and congressional tax-writing committees were concerned about what they saw as a "loophole" in the area of charitable giving. The problem had to do with gifts to charity of "appreciated property," generally, that is, property that had increased in value since the donor acquired it.

Prior to 1986, when a taxpayer gave appreciated property to charity, the resulting charitable deduction was generally for the *full fair market value of the gift* (subject to limitations discussed earlier in this book). In other words, critics of this provision noted, the donor not only didn't have to pay any tax on the increase in value, but even worse (it was argued) the donor could use that increase in value as part of a tax deduction, to shelter or offset income.

The benefits can be dramatic. Let's say John Landowner owns 1,000 shares of IBM stock that he purchased years ago at $20.00 per share. If John gives that IBM stock to his *alma mater* when the value is $100.00 per share, John has a *$100,000 income tax deduction for what was once a $20,000 outlay.* It didn't sit well with some in Washington that this pleasant tax-planning opportunity continued to be available to John and countless others like him.

The charitable lobby, which is strong and well organized, was able to fight back attempts over the years to modify this provision (or close this loophole, as some argued). In the Tax Reform Act of 1986, however, Congress made significant changes in this area of the tax code, and those changes are today an integral part of tax planning for land conservation gifts.

In 1992 Congress was almost successful in repealing the alternative minimum tax rule for charitable gifts. However, the tax bill including the repeal provision was vetoed.

As noted earlier in this book, at this writing it is anticipated that Congress may try again to repeal this rule in 1993 or 1994. What this means is that if you are thinking seriously about making a charitable gift of an easement, or of land, or of any other appreciated property, you must consult with an advisor to determine what the effect of the AMT might be on your personal situation and *also to find out whether the AMT still applies at all to your contemplated gift!!*

This Appendix covers the mechanics of the AMT and includes some examples to illustrate the sometimes unpredictable effect of the AMT. At the very end of this Appendix, I have included a brief section on the few (but important) changes in the earlier chapters of this book that you will want to know about *if the AMT is repealed.*

Some Points to Keep in Mind

A few important points before we get to the rules.

The way the AMT works mechanically is that many taxpayers will have to figure their regular income tax liability, then figure their alternative minimum tax liability, then *pay whichever is higher.* The first point to keep in mind is that *it is safe to assume that someone who makes a charitable contribution of appreciated property will not end up paying more in income taxes because of the alternative minimum tax than if the gift had never been made in the first place.*

In other words, the AMT *may reduce the income tax savings* from such a charitable gift but *should never penalize you* with a higher tax than if you had not made the gift at all. All three Examples below (as well as the Examples in Chapter 3) illustrate this point.

Second, in many cases the AMT will have *absolutely*

no effect or very little effect on the income tax benefits or savings from charitable gifts. See Example 1 and Example 2 below.

Third, it is impossible to provide *generalized* tax planning advice about the AMT that will be useful in *individual* situations. If you are thinking about making a gift of appreciated property to charity, you must seek *individual, professional tax advice for your own particular situation.*

Fourth, *even if* the AMT rules severely reduce the otherwise available *income tax savings* from a conservation gift, the *estate tax benefits* may be of far greater importance. As I discussed in earlier chapters, highly appreciated family land may create a serious problem for an estate; a conservation easement, even without significant income tax benefits, may be a significant and appropriate estate planning tool.

Fifth, for some people confronted with the AMT, certain planning techniques may be helpful. If, for example, you can *accelerate income* into the year or years when you are subject to the AMT, the news may not even be all bad. *Check with your advisor.*

The AMT Rules

Recall that (as noted above) the way the AMT works mechanically is that many taxpayers will have to figure their regular income tax liability, then figure their alternative minimum tax liability, *then pay whichever is higher.*

Very simply put, the AMT rule on gifts of appreciated property to charity works like this. Although you may deduct the full fair market value of the gift in figuring your *regular income tax liability*, for *alternative minimum tax purposes* you may effectively deduct *only* the cost (or basis) of the gift (generally, what you paid for the property); that is, for alternative minimum tax purposes you may not deduct the amount represented by the appreciation (the increase in the property's value over its tax cost or basis). (Technically, in the calculation of the AMT, what happens is that the full value of the gift is first deducted from taxable income and then the "appreciation" portion is added back.)

As it originally passed Congress in 1986, this rule covered the gift of *any* appreciated property to *any* charity. That is, it covered the gift of appreciated IBM stock to the *alma mater*, or the gift of a painting to a museum, or the gift of land, or of a conservation easement, to a tax-exempt conservation organization.

Because of later Congressional amendments, during 1991 and part of 1992 the AMT rule did not apply to *certain* gifts, such as the gift of a painting or valuable antiques to a museum. At the end of 1992, as noted above, a tax bill passed Congress that included (among other things) a *permanent repeal* of the AMT in connection with charitable gifts. Because that bill was vetoed, however, at this writing the AMT now applies, once again, to any gift of appreciated property to any charity.

As a result, it continues to be important to understand how the AMT works.

"Basis" and "Appreciation"

Before going to the Examples to illustrate the possible effect (or lack of effect) of the AMT, two technical points are important. As I mentioned above, while the cost or basis (what you paid for the property) remains fully deductible under the AMT calculations, the appreciation portion (the increase in value) does not. If the asset being donated to charity is a share of stock, or a painting, or an outright gift of land, those two numbers (cost and appreciation) are not difficult to determine. But how do we determine the "basis" of a conservation easement and the "appreciation" portion?

We need three pieces of information. First, we need to know the tax cost or basis of the underlying land itself. Second, we need to know the current fair market value of the land. Third, we need to know the value of the easement. Let's use an example to illustrate how we determine the answers to our questions.

Let's assume the basis of Riverview is $100,000 and the current value of Riverview is $500,000. And let's assume that an easement reduces the value of Riverview to $300,000 (so the easement is worth $200,000). Because the easement represents 40% of the value of Riverview ($200,000/$500,000), under the tax rules 40% of Riverview's $100,000 basis, or $40,000, becomes the "basis" of the easement (or, is "allocated" to the easement). The "balance" of the easement's value, or $160,000 ($200,000 minus $40,000), becomes the "appreciation" portion *for purposes of the AMT.*

The rule is purely mechanical: whatever percentage of the *property's value* is represented by the easement, a similar percentage of the *basis* is "allocated" to the easement.

This is a highly technical tax rule that relies on two highly technical assumptions, that the "value" of the easement is equal to the value of Riverview's development rights and that basis can be divided up in such a manner. But this is the first rule we need to know to be prepared to look at the effect of the AMT.

More useful information is also available if we follow this example a little further. Because of the $40,000 out of the total $100,000 basis that is "allocated" to the *easement*, the remaining basis of *Riverview itself* is reduced to $60,000 ($100,000 minus $40,000). If Riverview is some day sold, subject to the easement, for $150,000, John and Mary will have $90,000 of gain ($150,000 minus Riverview's basis of $60,000).

Deduct Basis First

Following the above example, we have an easement valued at $200,000 with a basis of $40,000.

Remember from Chapter 3 the rule that the value of a charitable gift may be deducted up to 30% of the donor's income. Let's assume that John and Mary have income of $100,000 and they donate the easement to a charitable conservation organization. The easement is worth $200,000, their income is $100,000; the deduction is $30,000 (30% of $100,000).

The $170,000 balance of the gift ($200,000 minus $30,000) "carries forward" and can be used against John and Mary's income for the next five years.

	Year 1	Year 2	Year 3	Year 4	Year 5	Year 6
Income	$100,000	$100,000	$100,000	$100,000	$100,000	$100,000
Easement Deduction	30,000	30,000	30,000	30,000	30,000	30,000

This is all we need to know for *income tax deduction* purposes. But for alternative minimum tax purposes, we need to know how much of the gift is "basis" and how much is "appreciation."

Recall that this easement gift has a "basis" of $40,000. *The Internal Revenue Service has issued a rule that states that for AMT purposes, the "basis" portion of the gift is deducted first, before deducting the appreciation.* Looking at this rule as it applies to our example, this is what we see.

	Year 1	Year 2	Year 3	Year 4	Year 5	Year 6
Income	$100,000	$100,000	$100,000	$100,000	$100,000	$100,000
Easement Deduction	30,000	30,000	30,000	30,000	30,000	30,000
"Basis" portion of Deduction	30,000	10,000	0	0	0	0
"Appreciation" portion of Deduction	0	20,000	30,000	30,000	30,000	30,000

Now, let's see what this means in terms of income tax savings from the deduction. Note from the tables below that when the $30,000 charitable deduction is all basis (in Year 1), there is no alternative minimum tax effect (because the regular tax rate and the tax are higher). In Year 2, with the $30,000 charitable deduction made up of $10,000 of basis and $20,000 of appreciation, there is a *small* AMT effect. And in Years 3-6, when the $30,000 charitable deduction is all appreciation, there is a larger AMT effect.

But also note, *and this is very important,* even though the $30,000 charitable deduction in Years 3-6 is all appreciation, and even though there is an AMT effect in each of those years, the charitable gift *still results in income tax savings.* (See also Example 3 later in this Appendix.) Without the gift, in those years the tax due each year would have been $18,138; with the gift, *and even with the AMT,* the tax due is $12,840.

For purposes of these calculations, assume that John and Mary also have deductions of $5,000 for state income tax, $2,500 for property tax, and $6,500 in mortgage interest.

Without the Donation

	Years 1-6
Income	$100,000
Deductions	14,000
Tax Due	18,138

With the Donation

	Year 1	Year 2	Years 3-6
Income	$100,000	$100,000	$100,000
Deductions	44,000	44,000	44,000
Regular Tax	9,738	9,738	9,738
AMT	5,640	10,440	12,840
Tax Due	9,738	10,440	12,840

What does this tell us about the subtle but important rule that basis is deducted first? First, assuming the gift has some significant amount of basis, in the first year or years the gift is deductible you may not have to worry about the AMT *at all*. Second, it is at least a possibility that if there are *no* AMT consequences in the first year of such a gift, there *may be* AMT consequences in future years (when all of the basis has been deducted and the remaining deduction is entirely appreciation); see Example 3 below for another illustration of this point. Third, and I'm going to repeat myself, it is impossible to provide *generalized* tax planning advice here that will be useful in *individual* situations. Any taxpayer contemplating a gift of appreciated property to charity must seek individual, professional advice on tax planning for his or her own particular situation.

Some Examples

Example 1

John and Mary have a combined annual income of $70,000; they have $10,000 in deductions ($3,500 in state income tax and $6,500 in mortgage interest). They donate to a conservation organization an easement with a value of $50,000 and a basis of $10,000. Note that the $50,000 deduction is fully deducted, or "used up," after three years.

Without the Donation

	Years 1-3
Income	$70,000
Deductions	10,000
Tax Due	10,858

With the Donation

	Year 1	Year 2	Year 3
Income	$70,000	$70,000	$70,000
Deductions	31,000	31,000	18,000
Regular Tax	5,160	5,160	8,618
AMT	3,240	5,640	5,640
Tax Due	5,160	5,640	8,618

Total tax due over Years 1-3 *without* the easement donation: $32,574

Total tax due over Years 1-3 *with* the easement donation: $19,418

Income Tax Savings: $13,156

Note the alternative minimum tax has a small effect, only in Year 2!!

Example 2

John and Mary Landowner have $225,000 in adjusted gross income and $45,000 in other deductions (assume $10,000 in state income tax and $35,000 in mortgage interest on their first and second homes). The value of the gift (whether an easement or an outright gift of land) is $75,000. Of that amount, $40,000 is basis and $35,000 is appreciation. Here, the $75,000 deduction is used up in two years.

Without the Donation

	Years 1-2
Income	$225,000
Deductions	41,407
Tax Due	49,009

With the Donation

	Year 1	Year 2
Income	$225,000	$225,000
Deductions	108,907	48,907
Regular Tax	28,084	46,684
AMT	26,400	38,400
Tax Due	28,084	46,684

Total tax due over Years 1 and 2 *without* the donation: $98,018

Total tax due over Years 1 and 2 *with* the donation: $74,768

Income Tax Savings: $23,250

Note that the alternative minimum tax has no effect.

Example 3

John and Mary have an income of $500,000 and deductions of $65,000 ($20,000 in state income tax and $45,000 in mortgage interest). They contribute an easement that is worth $1,000,000 to a conservation organization. The basis of the easement is determined to be $250,000. These are the results:

Without the Donation

	Years 1-4	Years 5-6
Income	$500,000	$500,000
Deductions	53,157	65,000
Tax Due	131,272	126,175

With the Donation

	Year 1	Year 2	Years 3-4	Years 5-6
Income	$500,000	$500,000	$500,000	$500,000
Deductions	203,157	203,157	203,157	215,000
Regular Tax	84,772	84,772	84,772	79,675
AMT	72,900	85,200	109,200	109,200
Tax Due	84,772	85,200	109,200	109,200

Total tax due over Years 1-6 *without* the easement donation: $777,438

Total tax due over Years 1-6 *with* the easement donation: $606,772

Income Tax Savings: $170,666

What is interesting about Example 3 is that the alternative minimum tax has no effect in the first year but then (barely) kicks in beginning in Year 2. Again, this is because of the IRS rule that basis is deductible first, before deducting appreciation, and in this Example the $250,000 basis was fully deductible in the first two years.

Note something else in Example 3 that is *very significant.* In Years 3-6, the deduction carried forward from the charitable gift was entirely *appreciation,* since the entire *basis* of the gift had previously been deducted. In Years 3-6, *without the gift,* the total tax due would be $514,894; in Years 3-6, with the gift and *even though the gift at this point is all appreciation,* the total tax due is reduced to $436,800. *This clearly illustrates, once again, that even if the deduction from a charitable gift is all appreciation, there still may be some considerable income tax benefit.* The moral of this story? Don't generalize about the AMT! Run the numbers!

Finally, of course, remember that we are talking about more than income tax benefits. In this example, the combination of the *income tax benefits and the significant potential estate tax benefits* (achieved by reducing the value of Riverview by $1,000,000) make a conservation easement an important family tax and land-planning tool for the Landowners.

Comments and Observations

The alternative minimum tax is something your tax attorney or accountant will have to compute for you. This Appendix simply illustrates what is involved and that the AMT cannot be overlooked in the planning process.

One thing that the Examples in this Appendix do not illustrate is that if your tax attorney or accountant "runs the numbers" and determines that the AMT will reduce the income tax benefits from your charitable gift, there are some steps you can take to plan for or around the AMT. You can, for example, make smaller gifts, or, if you have the flexibility, you can accelerate additional taxable income into the year of the gift. (A discussion of AMT planning is beyond the scope of this work. Your advisor should be able to help you with this, however.)

If the AMT is Repealed

The results of the "John and Mary" example in Chapter 3 will change. Without an alternative minimum tax, their income tax savings will be more than $50,000 greater over six years.

The results of the "Bob and Sue" example in Chapter 3 will not change, since in that example Bob and Sue didn't have to worry about the AMT anyway.

The results of good tax planning for John and Mary in Chapter 7 get even better. That chapter considered what would happen if John and Mary used a conservation easement to protect Riverview and reserved some lots for limited development, rather than selling out for cash. The results get better simply because the income tax savings from the easement donation increase substantially.

Without an alternative minimum tax, tax planning for charitable contributions of appreciated property will become easier and income tax benefits from charitable contributions of appreciated property will often (though certainly not always) increase.

And, of course, without an alternative minimum tax you can ignore the rest of this Appendix C.

Tax Planning for Charitable Gifts – A Special Rule

A Special Rule

Congress has provided a special rule in the tax code having to do with charitable gifts of appreciated property. In many situations, taking advantage of this rule will be of no use to a donor and will not save any money. But in *some* situations *this might be the smart choice to make.*

Remember that under the *general* rule, a taxpayer who makes a charitable contribution of property can deduct the value of that gift up to 30% of income. Under the *special* rule, a taxpayer who makes a charitable gift of appreciated property *can choose to reduce the amount of the deduction to the cost or basis of the property,* and two new rules will follow.

First, the value of the gift (as reduced to basis) will be deductible *up to 50% of the taxpayer's income,* compared to the 30% ceiling without the special rule. Second, *none of the deduction will be subject to the alternative minimum tax.*

The decision to use the new rule is made by making an "election" to reduce the value of the gift to basis, and to increase the deduction to 50% of income. The "election" is made on a statement filed with your tax return. Your advisor can help you with the details.

When to Consider the Special Rule: Little or No Appreciation

In certain situations, it seems clear that making the election may be the right thing to do. One such situation occurs when a gift of property or of an easement is made either shortly after acquiring the property, either by purchase or inheritance (when there has been a "stepped-up basis," as discussed in Chapter 7), or when there has not been any significant increase in the value of the property. But don't assume anything!! Run the numbers!!

Example 1

In January, 1990, John and Mary acquire Riverview for $390,000. In February, 1992, when Riverview is valued at $420,000, John and Mary donate an easement that lowers the value of Riverview to $280,000. The value of the easement is $140,000, and its basis is $130,000 (one-third of Riverview's basis of $390,000).

John and Mary have annual income of $120,000 and other deductions of $35,000 ($10,000 in state income tax and $25,000 in mortgage interest). The $140,000 easement deduction is used up in four years.

Without the Donation

	Years 1-4
Income	$120,000
Deductions	34,557
Tax Due	17,982

With the Donation and Without the Election

	Years 1-3	Year 4
Income	$120,000	$120,000
Deductions	70,557	66,557
Regular Tax	7,902	9,022
AMT	4,560	7,920
Tax Due	7,902	9,022

With the Donation and With the Election

	Years 1-2	Year 3	Year 4
Income	$120,000	$120,000	$120,000
Deductions	94,557	44,557	34,557
Regular Tax	3,126	15,182	17,982
AMT	-0-	10,800	13,200
Tax Due	3,126	15,182	17,982

Income Tax Savings, Without Election: $39,200

Income Tax Savings, With Election: $32,512

Note that with the election the tax savings are significantly higher in the first two years. Once again, *this example illustrates the importance of running the numbers and the value of good planning.*

Example 2

A similar opportunity to accelerate the income tax savings exists in the case of the "conservation buyer" or "country buyer," the buyer who is willing to pay a premium for a valuable piece of land but who does not want to develop that land. The buyer may be someone who has had an enormously successful financial year, from a rock star to a lottery winner, or any other wealthy individual who can afford to pay top dollar.

Let's assume Mr. Entrepreneur, whose annual income is normally in the $200,000 to $400,000 a year range, has just sold a block of stock in the company he began ten years ago, and his taxable income this year jumps to $3,500,000. Mr. and Mrs. Entrepreneur buy Riverview, John and Mary's 200-acre estate, for $2,500,000. Mr. and Mrs. Entrepreneur then donate a conservation easement on Riverview, prohibiting any further development, and the value of Riverview is reduced to $1,000,000.

Since there has been no increase in the value of Riverview since Mr. and Mrs. Entrepreneur acquired it, *all* $1,500,000 of the deduction is basis. Mr. and Mrs. Entrepreneur make the election, and these are the results for the year of the donation (assume no other deductions):

Without the Donation

	Year 1
Income	$3,500,000
Tax	982,891

With the Donation and the Election
Year 1

Income	$3,500,000
Deduction	1,398,157
Tax	583,862

Income Tax Savings: $399,029

It does not matter whether Mr. and Mrs. Entrepreneur are motivated by a strong conservation ethic or by tax savings or both. The result is the same in either case. A wealthy buyer with a significant amount of taxable income can help "finance" the acquisition of desirable property in this manner; a "conservation buyer" can acquire a sensitive and important piece of land that comes on the market, land that perhaps is being sold by an estate (before the property owner had a chance to read this book), and can help "finance" the protection of that land with this same technique.

When Else to Consider the Election

There are a lot of variables involved in tax planning. It is often difficult to generalize about when to make the election and sometimes it is unwise to generalize. But it often makes sense simply to run the numbers to determine whether some additional income tax savings would be available with the election. One specific situation in which the election should be considered is when the donors (or donor) are quite elderly or in such poor health that the potential benefits of a five-year carryforward of the income tax deduction may never be realized.

The following example illustrates the case of an elderly donor and also illustrates some of the variables, and some of the choices, involved in tax planning.

Example 3

Mary Landowner is 85 and a widow. She has a large annual income from investments and $25,000 in deductions ($15,000 in state income tax, $5,000 in property tax, and $5,000 in mortgage interest). Let's assume in this case that Riverview has a basis of $550,000 and is currently valued at $1,000,000. Let's also assume that an easement prohibiting any further development on Riverview would be valued at $500,000 and would therefore have a basis of $275,000 (50% of Riverview's basis of $550,000).

Without the Donation

	Years 1-4	Years 5-6
Income	$300,000	$300,000
Deductions	19,157	25,000
Tax Due	82,716	80,192

With the Donation and Without the Election

	Years 1-3	Year 4	Year 5	Year 6
Income	$300,000	$300,000	$300,000	$300,000
Deductions	109,157	109,157	115,000	75,000
Regular Tax	54,816	54,816	52,292	64,692
AMT	47,550	69,600	70,800	70,800
Tax Due	54,816	69,600	70,800	70,800

With the Donation and With the Election

	Year 1	Year 2	Years 3-4	Years 5-6
Income	$300,000	$300,000	$300,000	$300,000
Deductions	169,157	144,157	19,157	25,000
Regular Tax	36,216	43,966	82,716	80,192
AMT	29,550	37,050	70,800	70,800
Tax Due	36,216	43,966	82,716	80,192

Income Tax Savings, Without Election: $115,600

Income Tax Savings, With Election: $85,250

Income Tax Savings, Years 1-2, Without Election: $55,800

Income Tax Savings, Years 1-2, With Election: $85,250

The numbers speak for themselves. In this situation, of course, the decision whether or not to make the election is a particularly personal one for each donor.

Comments and Observations

Once again, as with most of the other tax consequences of charitable conservation giving, generalizations can only go so far. Further, what makes sense with the same income and deductions each year may not make sense if a landowner expects significant financial changes from one year to the next. Clearly, there is no substitute for good counsel and for "running the numbers." The election may be useful and appropriate only in certain circumstances, but it is up to each donor to determine whether his or her situation is one of them.

ABOUT THE AUTHOR

Stephen J. Small is a tax attorney at his own firm, the Law Office of Stephen J. Small, Esq., in Boston. He is the author of *The Federal Tax Law of Conservation Easements* (Land Trust Alliance, 1985) and *Preserving Family Lands* (first edition self-published, 1988). The first edition of *Preserving Family Lands* sold more than 50,000 copies.

Before going into private practice, Mr. Small was an attorney-advisor in the Office of Chief Counsel of the Internal Revenue Service in Washington, D.C., where he wrote the federal income tax regulations on conservation easements.

Mr. Small currently works with landowners and their advisors on federal income and estate tax planning to help preserve valued family land, including planning for the next generation of ownership. He has worked with private landowners around the country to preserve a wide range of property, from small family parcels, timberland, and dairy farms in the northeast to western ranches, Atlantic coast barrier islands, and farmland and wildlife habitat in the southeast.

Since 1988, Mr. Small has given more than one hundred speeches, seminars, and workshops around the country on tax planning for landowners and tax incentives for land conservation. He is a member of the Massachusetts and District of Columbia Bars.

If you would like information about other publications, or if you would like to be on our mailing list to be notified about future Landowner Planning Center material, please write to:

Landowner Planning Center
P.O. Box 4508
Boston, MA 02101-4508
(617) 357-1644